Author's Note

I was diagnosed with Parkinson's Disease in February 2018, and looking back, the worst thing about it was being told. As I journey with this new unwanted guest in my life, I have begun to understand the disease more, and together with Bridget, my wife, we manage it (and the challenges it brings) on a daily basis.

Most people think that Parkinson's Disease is all about tremors and shuffles when we walk. However, there are more than 40 symptoms associated with Parkinson's Disease and here are just a few. They can be as diverse as a loss or reduction of the sense of smell, a lack of facial expression (flat face), apathy, depression, constipation, muscle stiffness, loss of balance, problems walking, insomnia, vivid nightmares, slurred speech and loss of voice volume. A combination of any or all of these can lead to anxiety, loss of confidence and depression. It has been said that when you meet one person with Parkinson's you've met one person with Parkinson's. We're all different, yet we all have symptoms in common. In an interview in the Washington Post, long-term sufferer and Parkinson's campaigner Michael J Fox said, "You don't die from Parkinson's, you die with it," which is a good thing, I suppose.

But the biggest plus is that many Parkinson's sufferers – possibly through a combination of their condition and medication – become quite creative. I always wrote little rhymes in family birthday cards and on special occasions, as did my father and his father before him. However, since diagnosis my poetry has developed and become quite prolific. I write daily about all kinds of subjects and experiences and get an enormous amount of joy from it as, dare I say, the people I write it for.

So, with the help of Bridget, and my good friend Pete Norman (who although he doesn't have PD, still writes some very profound and entertaining verse), we have taken what we feel are the best pieces. Here they are. We hope you enjoy them.

PARKINSON'S POEMS

These first few poems are about Parkinson's Disease and how I felt about it at the time of writing.

I find writing about my condition a cathartic exercise and try not to get too obsessed with it. Life goes on and there are lots of other topics to explore and write about.

Parkinson's Disease Two Views

Written September 2020

Eighteen months since I was diagnosed
With Parkinson's, and told it grows.
Slow, or fast, it will get worse.
Yes, at first, quite a shock
To experience the ticking of that clock,
And feeling that it was a curse.

But, as time has now moved on,
The initial shock has gone,
And I've settled into a new regime.
Count my blessings, that by my side
Is Bridget, when bumpy gets the ride.
And there is an upside – or so it seems.

As I take my daily drug,
I can only sit and shrug,
Ponder what it's doing to me.
Compulsive behaviour, a side effect,
Something I really did not expect,
And expressing my thoughts in poetry.

With all its shams and broken dreams
The world is still lovelier than it sometimes seems.
No matter what you're facing,
Nothing lasts forever,
It changes like the weather,
That rainbow's still worth chasing.

Written March 2023

I have a disease, it's called PD.
It's not obvious, for all to see.
My thoughts they turn to verse.
A blessing it gives me, not a curse.
We're a partnership, PD and Me.

Last Night I had a Dream

Last night I had a dream.
So real, so real it seemed.
And whatever it meant,
This dream that I dreamt.
It filled me with negativity,
It invaded my sensitivity.
Being treated, oh, so bad.
I felt rejected, I felt sad.
Awake, and this feeling stayed,
As in my bed I laid.
So, I arise from my bed.
And, to try and clear my head,
I write thoughts down in verse.
It has to be the first
Task that I was needing
To do; clear this feeling,
The images still in my head,
Of what I dreamt whilst still in bed.
But now they start to fade.
The images my mind had made.
No longer so real does it seem
Last night I had a dream.

Insomnia

Everyone has gone to bed,
But I am not alone; instead
The company that's left for me,
Is Parkinson's, inside my head.

The sandman's knocking on my door,
Parkinson's says, "Not anymore.
Sleep I will deny, even though you try,
It will not wash upon your shore.

I am now your unwelcome guide,
A seat for you, you're on my ride."
I contemplate my fate as it gets late,
And how I might stem this tide.

"You've won the battle, but not the war,
I'll win the day, fight tooth and claw.
Take my sleep, it's yours to keep."
Now, in your face, I'll slam that door.

The Horns of Uncertainty

You're impaled upon the horns of uncertainty,
Climbing a wall that can never be scaled.
Surfing a wave you don't want to ride,
Bound by ropes that can't be untied.
Navigating a sea you've never before sailed.

Parkinson's! A Multitude of symptoms,
Each an adversary you're trying to fight.
All of us different, but also the same,
Shakers United playing the same game.
But not ninety minutes – there is no respite.

Again! Again! Again and again,
Each day a challenge and so you begin.
Start the day and hope for the best,
First the tedium of trying to get dressed.
On with the fight that you'll never win.

But carry on, as there's no other choice,
Keep your head above water and try not to drown.
Sleep if you can - but then there's the dreams,
Nightmares and panic and occasional screams.
You wake and get up, but it's getting you down.

An uninvited guest who won't go away,
His company something I now have to keep.
He won't kill me, but he'll stay to the end,
Wearing me down I cannot pretend,
So, into the unknown I continue to leap.

No Choice

My first attempt at a villanelle.
A villanelle is a 19-line poem that follows a specific structure and rhyme scheme. It is
made up of five tercets (stanzas with three lines) and a quatrain (stanza with four lines)

I sit and take my daily drug,
It's now my new routine.
From under my feet it's pulled the rug.

No choice, I give a shrug.
Parkinson's you are so mean.
I sit and take my daily drug.

Bad days, please, I need a hug.
On you I need to lean.
From under my feet it's pulled the rug.

Now part of the PD club,
No quick fix, or vaccine.
I sit and take my daily drug.

Nightmares, or bad dreams,
More symptoms, so it seems.
I sit and take my daily drug.
From under my feet it's pulled the rug.

Living the Dream

In my dream, my health exudes
With youth and long-forgotten vigour.
Parkinson's cannot intrude
In this world, he does not figure.
But there I cannot long remain
As dawn invades my space.
Inevitably I must try again
To put a smile on this blank face.
Take that first unstable stride
Hear those words, "You're looking good!"
No, it's just that I can hide
And surely would do if I could.

Relatively Speaking

Relatively speaking, I'm healthy and fit,
But with Parkinson's Disease I still feel like shit.
I know other afflictions are a lot worse,
I know I'm not stuck in a bed or a chair.
I have a choice, indoors or fresh air.
But PD is still a real curse.

I'm not lonely, a loving wife and good friends,
Not many worries or many loose ends.
But energy levels are sapped every day,
Drop food on the floor, the dog is well-pleased.
Fell over again, another scrape on my knees.
Getting dressed I can cause a delay.

I dribble, I'm clumsy, no facial expression,
Can't remember the answer when I'm asked a question.
Relatively speaking, I'm healthy and fit.
Feel nauseous in the morning, 'til breakfast is fixed.
Shove pills down my throat, it's still only six.
With Parkinson's Disease I still feel like shit.

Speaking Relatively

Speaking relatively, I'm healthy and fit,
Have Parkinson's Disease, but only a bit.
Short tennis, table tennis, two weekly sports,
Backgammon and chess, dog walking – of sorts.
Bridge with some friends, my days are all free.
A home that I love out in the country.
A garden I enjoy, growing the veg.
Gone are the days of living life on the edge.
Children have grown and are all doing well,
Got grandchildren too, all happy as well.
As wife that I love and who loves me too.
Without her I'd be right in the poo.
Speaking relatively, I'm healthy and fit.
Have Parkinson's Disease, but only a bit.

HUMOUROUS

So now let's lighten things up a bit. This next section makes me laugh and hopefully one or two of them will bring a smile to your face too.

Mersey Heartbeat

Liverpool in the sixties and it's really swinging.
Crossing the Mersey on the ferry,
You might hear someone who's singing.
And if you're lucky, it could be Gerry.

Gerry and his band The Pacemakers
Were creating new music scenes.
With Lulu and The Beatles they were really shakers
For all of us in our teens.

Now sixty years have passed us by,
They no longer sound their best.
Because, and I will tell you why,
The pacemaker's now in their chest!

Some Things

There are some things that you talk about,
And some things that you don't.
Some things that you will accept,
And some things that you won't.

Erectile dysfunction, a dried-up tush,
A leaky bladder, or an itchy bush,
An unwelcome sting, an itchy ring,
Constipation, and a real need to push.

Night-time sweats, uncontrollable farts,
Varicose veins and replacement parts.
Put your teeth in a glass, at night you can't sleep.
Can't give them back, they're all yours to keep.

That's just a few I've mentioned to you.
I'm sure you'll admit to none.
But if you don't have them now,
They'll get you somehow,
Long before your day is done.

Gone Away

Time is running short,
I thought that you should know,
That it won't be very long
Before it's time for me to go.

Keep the car in the garage,
I don't want to sound too mean,
But please look after the garden,
And keep the house all clean.

And if you find anything,
That you feel I have forgot,
Don't worry about it too much,
It won't worry me a lot.

Because I'll be gone far away,
Leaving you all behind.
Please look after my little dog
And treat him very kind.

So, when I come back from my holiday,
Refreshed and with a tan,
I'll find everything in order,
That's the kind of guy I am!

W.O.R.D.L.E

I have now become committed,
And find that I am addicted,
Each day another hurdle,
As I play a game called W.O.R.D.L.E.

So, now where shall I start?
The first word I try is G.R.A.C.E.
Only the E fits,
But not in the right place.

I follow on with P.I.E.T.Y,
That is my second try.
Not that bad a choice.
I now have the E and I.

P.R.I.M.E is the next word I choose.
The R and I are set.
The E is still not in its place.
This is not over yet!

Already three guesses have gone,
So, B.R.I.N.E I place in haste.
I forgot to move the E!
That turn was just a waste.

I'm now on move number five,
P.R.I.D.E has to be what's needed.
I forgot to move the E again!
Still, I've not succeeded.

Last chance, tentatively I put F.R.I.E.D.
It's wrong. Defeat I must admit.
How stupid, how I nearly C.R.I.E.D
That I didn't think of it.

Superstition

Some people do believe them,
Some say they're superstitious.
Some people are deceived by them,
These age-old held traditions.

Pick a four-leaf clover,
Kiss the Blarney Stone.
Throw salt over your shoulder,
Pull a chicken's wishing bone.

Blow out the candles in one breath,
A silent wish – don't tell!
Do the same upon a star,
Or throw a coin into a well.

A rabbit's paw on a key ring,
Is it just a funny habit?
It didn't bring a lot of luck
To that poor bunny rabbit!

Under a ladder, but cross your fingers,
Expect money with an itchy palm.
Don't put new shoes upon the table,
Friday 13th – you must stay calm.

Seven years' bad luck when you break a glass,
You'll forget it by next week.
Unless, of course, the one you broke
Was grandma's best antique.

Now, I don't believe this nonsense,
And you might also have a laugh,
But I'm staying in the house today
Because a black cat crossed my path.

Hats

If you want to get ahead, get a hat.
Churchill's homburg, you'd cut a dash wearing that,
A balmoral bonnet on an invite from the King,
A tam o'shanter when dancing a fling,
A bearskin for trooping the colour,
A green beret for showing patriotic valour,
A boater for punting down on the river,
A balaclava to ensure you don't ever shiver,
A mortar board was for when you graduated,
A bowler? No! It's far too outdated,
Be Davy Crockett and put on a coonskin,
A montera to face a bull in the bullring,
A hard hat for when you're working on site,
A headlamp for when you're out late at night,
I've not mentioned a pork pie or turban, somebrero, fedora or fez,
A beanie would suit a suburban,
A stetson if you lived in Cortez,
There's a hat for every occasion,
Even if it's only a cap,
So, check out a style that will suit you,
If you want to get ahead, get a hat!

Shakespearean Omelette

Brevity is the source of wit,
So, as I write this recipe
Please do not think less of me
If I go on a bit.

Do not borrow, or even lend
Use what there is to hand.
The ingredients that you use
Will dictate the size of pan.

To thine own self be true
Adopt this recipe.
As night will follow day
To be or not to be.

Crack them open,
Down they fall,
Alas, dear yolk
I knew him well!

Add milk and seasoning to taste
Altogether you now fry.
Do I hear you cry out loud?
All that lives must surely die.

To you I'm cruel, to me you're kind,
But that always was your fate.
Silent now, as it's all done
And you're lying there upon my plate.

Not onions or garlic did Shakespeare add
Whilst sitting in company.
So, he might, with sweet breath
And hear sweet comedy.

STORIES

I've written a few children's stories (in rhyme) and discovered that story writing is my favourite genre. I can let my imagination just run away with itself. I find an inspiring opening line and then just let it run.

Me and Mr Mole

The vegetable garden, not just a place to grow
Vegetables and flowers to show.
But a place of endless activity.
A joy to watch in every corner,
Hard at work, flower and fauna.
But underground where we can't see,
Lives a gardener's adversary.

Squirrels, pigeons and Cabbage White,
Some of the garden residents that might
Do damage in their daily task.
But, although I try, I cannot pardon,
The one who lives under my garden.
A request too much to ask.

Now I have become obsessed.
And find myself put to the test,
To catch this little creature
Who spends his nights and days
In secret underground highways,
The elusive Talpa Europaea.

It's now become a daily chore,
To try harder and do more and more.
To achieve what is my ultimate goal.
I'm sure, by now, you've worked it out.
There can really be no doubt
I must catch this European Grey Mole.

Today, at the rising of the sun,
It's paid off – the work I've done –
In trying to catch this wily beast.
For in the run the trap was laid.
Sure as that setting sun would fade,
Talpa Europaea would be deceased.

Lifting him out of the ground,
Lying in my palm, I confess, I found
A pretty, little handsome soul.
Myself feeling a little sad.
Having no choice, I really had
To end the life of this grey mole.

The feelings I had were bittersweet.
Enjoying my victory, sad for his defeat,
But pleased with the result of all my toil.
Where there is one there will be another,
And before long I did discover,
Those tell-tell signs – a mound of soil.

Disaster strikes! I thought I'd won,
But now it seems I've been undone.
Now must test this new foe's mettle.
Find the route that it takes,
Stop the damage that it makes.
I will not, cannot, let it settle!

So, I say to mole number two,
The struggle begins between me and you.
I set the trap into your run.
You're clever, I see you've changed your route.
But I'm on your case, in hot pursuit.
Your time has come, your day is done.

My victory, a short-lived narrative.
There's yet another relative
Careering through my vegetable patch.
How may are there? How many more?
I've won the battle, but not the war.
An endless column of foes to catch?

I'm on his turf – he has the edge.
It's my turf too – I'm on the edge
Of getting this out of all proportion.
Starting to affect my mental state.
Get a grip, for goodness' sake!
To myself I write this as a caution.

As I write this little rhyme.
Its cathartic words will, in time
Start to calm my disturbed soul.
Start to smile and start to reason.
It will end, like every season,
As I dig down through another hole.

Some battles you win and some you lose,
And, of course, you don't get to choose
The ones it will be.
So, one of us will win the day.
Who it will be, I cannot say.
We'll just have to wait and see.

There's been a contest between him and me.
This elusive mole, who's number three.
Created for his place, Oh, nature, so clever!
And taking on this uninvited challenge,
As above I will plan, and below he will scavenge.
Leave him be? The answer is, never!

Carrying on with my battle plan
The summer ends, see if I can
Still defeat this garden pest.
In tunnels deeper down below,
Lay the trap that will surely show
This mole defeat, when it leaves its nest.

The sun comes up and it's another day.
I'm tired of this, I have to say.
I wear a smile, no longer a frown,
As I give in and admit defeat
By a foe I will never meet,
But do admire and hand him the crown.

This change of thought, I wonder whether,
In harmony we might share together.
Accept that he just wants to live
And do what he does naturally,
Time for me to let him be.
Receive? Sometimes it's better just to give.

So, on you go, my new-found friend,
As I bring this poem to an end.
Pondering the journey as a whole.
And to think that you have shown me,
That we can live in harmony.
You clever, European grey mole.

A Year in the Life

Christmas has come and then it's gone.
Decorations down, that's all been done.
Now cold and wet, January has arrived.
Doesn't look nice, it's wet and grey.
No chance the sun will shine today.
But smile as I watch the buds survive.

February, and the days start to grow.
Snowdrops put on a welcome show.
Wind blows and bends the trees.
Light a fire, stay in, keep warm.
Spy some lambs, just been born.
The sun shines now and starts to tease.

Warmer days, promising what's to come.
March is here, here comes the sun.
Turn the ground, prepare the soil.
Anticipate the season ahead.
Garden comes to life, no longer dead.
Bounties of the earth, for which we toil.

Spirits rise, see shoulders lift,
As April brings its seasonal gift.
Longer days and life abounds.
Winter forgotten; spring is in the air.
Trees getting dressed, no longer bare.
Birds are busy, listen to nature's sounds.

Oh, the joy, we say hello to May.
Night now shorter than the day.
Smell the barbecue starting to cook.
Faces smile as our spirits lift,
As nature offers up its gift,
Giving back what winter took.

Long we've waited for the month of June.
Never seems to come too soon.
The sun is high, we bake.
Welcome now a warm, summer breeze.
Singing to us through the trees.
Blue skies, to another day we wake.

The sun is high up in the sky,
As we saunter on into July
Children playing, laughter abounds.
Now is the time for holidays.
Pack a bag, put cares away.
The air is full of joyous sounds.

August; complain about the heat.
Try to sleep under a sheet.
Where is the rain? Ground's too dry.
Walk along the esplanade.
Have a beer, seek some shade.
Had one salad too many you cry!

The bounties that September shows
Are found in blossoming hedgerows.
Days shorten, weather cools.
Wildlife will work much harder,
As they strive to fill their larder.
The season changes and nature rules.

October next to arrive.
Halloween, knock on the door, surprise!
Treats at the ready in the hall.
Wearing a sweater, a fire needs to be lit.
Warm yourself in front of it.
Leaves change their colour, and fall.

Crash and bang as fireworks fly!
Lighting up the winter sky.
Guess the month that we are in.
Start to think of presents to buy.
Time passes on so fast; you sigh.
Console yourself with tonic and gin.

Another year has been and gone,
With carols we sing a festive song.
We'll drink and eat too much you say,
Together people will celebrate,
From the birth of Christ to Christmas cake.
And it all starts again on New Years' Day!

My fried Pete and I would often get together to write and discuss poetry. One week we decided to take six well-known film phrases and each attempt to write a poetry story incorporating them all. A lot of fun, and this was my effort.

The phrases were:

"I've seen things you people wouldn't believe," from Blade Runner.
"I'm flying Jack, I'm flying," from Titanic.
"Of all the gin joints in all the towns in all the world," from Casablanca.
"It is a far, far better thing that I do today," from A Tale of Two Cities.
"I will find you, and when I do, I will kill you," from Taken.
"You're only supposed to blow the bloody doors off!" from The Italian Job.

Jack speaks, "I can be Jekyll, I can be Hyde.
I've seen things you people wouldn't believe.
And this is a job to make you all rich.
You can have wealth, that you couldn't conceive.

Simple, straightforward, we cannot lose.
Just do what I say, do as I ask.
Follow it through right down to the letter.
Do you have the nerve to take on this task?"

The task was to steal from a government vault.
Powder Pete set the dynamite, fixed to the door.
Everybody stepped back, the moment had come.
Pete set the fuse; it went off with a roar.

Jack screamed, "You're only supposed to blow
The bloody doors off!" he'd lost his calm.
The room was now filled with dust and smoke,
And the noise from a screeching alarm.

Powder Pete now scared, made his escape,
But the rest were caught for this piece.
"I will find you, and when I do, I will kill you!"
Was Jack's first thought on his early release.

Powder Pete had fled from the country,
But Jack had the man in his sight.
Hi girlfriend he took just for cover,
When at Heathrow they boarded a flight.

Now, Jill had not done any flying
This was her first time up in the sky.
"I'm flying Jack, I'm flying," she giggled.
Jack sat quietly and straightened his tie.

On arrival at their destination,
Jack said that he needed to go.
"Where?" said Jill with some consternation,
Jack retorted, "You don't need to know.

It is a far, far better thing I do today,"
Said Jack in a serious voice.
Revenge was all that he understood,
He really did not have a choice.

So Jack left the room, walked into the night,
And there in a dimly lit street
Was a bar called 'Everyman's Refuge'
And there in a corner, sat Powder Pete.

"Of all the gin joints, in all the towns, in all the world,"
Said Jack, "I've found you, and you cannot hide.
Do you recognize me Pete?" he smiled.
"Am I Dr Jekyll or am I Mr Hyde?"

Before Pete could give him an answer,
Jack pulled out from under his coat
A bone-handled knife (was his fathers')
And with it, slashed Powder Pete's throat.

Powder Pete – with a look of astonishment
Just making a gurgling sound.
Slid under the table he sat at,
In a pool of blood, on the ground.

Back in the hotel room, he tells Jill,
"If anyone asks you, I never left.
We stayed in and just watched a movie.
You had a headache and needed to rest."

But Jill was raised not to tell lies,
So when asked by the police the next day,
Told the truth and Jack was arrested.
What d'ya expect? Crime doesn't pay.

Lost

A long, winding stroll down a cold and windy beach
To a café that was closed, and you were out of reach.
An early start on an empty bus, paying a hopeful fare.
Each stop watching the people board, but sadly, you're not there.
A walk at the weekend on a busy shopping street,
Countless, faceless people, none of whom you wish to meet.
Standing in a closed shop doorway, you watch them passing by.
Take a tissue from your pocket, feel a tear fall from your eye.
Then, round the corner coming into view,
Is the one you've been searching for, who was made to be with you.
"Where have you been? I've been searching low and high,"
He wags his tail, gives a bark and licks the tear straight from my eye.

A few years ago, I joined Poets with Parkinson's, a group of fellow Parkinson's' sufferers who also write poetry. Each month we have a Zoom meeting where we collectively read our latest poems to each other. It is a wonderful and supportive group of like-minded friends. There is a monthly challenge to write a poem with a theme or containing a certain phrase. One month the phrase was – the beautiful cruel. The following is my effort. You can read more of the Poets with Parkinson's' work at poetswall.com.

The Beautiful Cruel

It was the 25th October 18 hundred and 54.
Young bloods had gathered with cheers and hurrahs.
Tomorrow they'd ride out with a gallop and a roar.
The proud 15th; the King's gallant hussars.

Robert spoke to John of his deepest fear.
"Now, don't be a coward. Wouldn't you rather
Ride with me? Swords drawn, together we'll cheer,
At dawn, in this place they call Balaclava."

As the sun rose on the following day,
All very quiet, they all felt the same.
Each man quietly to himself did pray.
Young men, just mere boys, honour to gain.

Maintaining their horses, in formation they stood.
Adrenaline high, in this they'd been trained.
Facing a valley in this barren land.
Kill or be killed, maim or be maimed.

Charge! And a gallop, off with a cry!
Six hundred young bloods thinking victory assured.
Not knowing that soon they would all die,
Into the valley they had been lured.

Cries and screams filled the hot air,
As boys fell and died in the heat.
Comrades together, these last hours they'd shared.
This day was the day their maker they'd meet.

In crimson uniform, with golden braid,
Life's blood shed under the sun.
Still and peaceful they now all laid,
And a mother grieved for the loss of her son.
Blood on his hands, you have to ask why?
The Earl of Cardigan, was he a fool?
To order his men, for their country to die?
For gallantry and honour – the beautiful cruel.

Sage Without Onion

Whilst walking in an everglade,
I met a sage of certain age,
And asked him why and how.

"Sit," he said, "just enjoy the now.
Speak and hear words you already know.
Listen instead and it might show
You something new, you never knew.
With careful thought a wise man speaks.
With none at all a fool just bleats."

These few words I sat and pondered,
Silence is golden, so I wondered.
Took his advice and sat quite still,
And waited for his words to fill
This still air and peaceful setting.
Excited what I might be getting.

Then from a tree a call I heard.
Announcing his presence, a tuneful bird.

The sage took a breath, "the bird is strong.
Those who sing will find a song.
Mistakes you'll make, don't be downcast,
Just use it as a lesson.
Guilt will not change the past,
But only ruin the present.
Forgive a child afraid of the dark,
Tragedy is a man who shuns the light."

A dog walked past and gave a bark.
Just saying hello, he will not bite.

"Enough for today, it's time to go."
The sage got up, nice and slow.
Turned to me and gave a bow.
Left me wondering why and how.

The Incident

You could hear a pin drop and the scurry of a mouse.
All was quiet, there was peace in this house.
The grandfather clock ticking, echoing down the hall.
The house had not been lived in since the incident at the ball.

A very grand occasion, and those who were invited,
Came adorned in best attire, clearly most excited.
The owner of the house, Major Reginald Trameer,
(A well-respected gentleman and a parliamentary peer).
The Major had two sons it was said they couldn't wait.
No love was lost between them, they both wanted the estate.

And on this night in question, there was a heated row,
The mother tried to stop it, but didn't quite know how.
A shot rang out from a gun and mother watched her favourite son
Fall to the ground and lay quite still, before her eyes his life blood spill.
She screamed at her other son, out of control, "What have you done?!"
In rage he turned, and with a yell, shot her too and down she fell.

The son was sentenced to life; the Major, inconsolable, had lost his wife.
So, some days later in the empty house, with his service pistol in his mouth,
A single tear fell from his eye, he pulled the trigger and said goodbye.
I leave all to charity, a note was read. If you read this, then I am dead.
A legal battle does now proceed, as money will manifest in greed.
Distant relatives fight for a slice, but the only occupants are the mice.

Midnight Rambler

The clock strikes twelve this winter's night.
From a heavy sky, down pours the rain.
Shoulders hunched and coat pulled tight,
My optimism starts to wane.

Thoughts in my head I now debate.
Why did I leave my safe abode?
Have I left it far too late,
Am I alone on this hostile road?

Lightning strikes, fleeting shadows cast,
I'm a grown man, I'm not a child,
I tell myself I must hold fast,
My imagination running wild.

But only once do I look behind,
Peer into the dark as I turn my head,
There's nothing there that I can find.
Does evil close behind me tread?

Superstition, but, if so, why?
Do I start to quicken my pace?
My heart rate quickens, my mouth runs dry,
What monster might I have to face?

A rancid odour fills the air,
Faster and faster, I start to run.
This creature tonight has left its lair,
Is this the end? A I undone?

Can see no rescue from my plight,
What ghastly beast could mutate,
And stalk its victims in the night?
Am I to face a grizzly fate?

I feel its grip, it's icy cold.
A slime upon my skin.
I struggle, but cannot break its hold,
I'm going to lose this beast will win.

My life is over, I'm approaching death,
I have one desperate choice.
I take my last, my deepest breath.
And at the very top of my voice
I scream my very loudest scream,
And wake up in bed in a cold sweat.
What a relief, it was just a dream,
And one I hope I'll soon forget.

Animal Farm

"Well muzzle my snout," said the pig to the shooter,
"I'd much prefer that to a ring through my hooter."
The bull looked up and mooed "I suppose,
You think I look daft with this ring through my nose?"
"Worse," grunted the pig "Just hark at these calls,
The lambs over there are losing their balls."
"Lost mine when a puppy, still in the pack.
Throw me a ball," barked the dog, "and I'll bring it right back."
"You think that that's bad", clucked the hen with a peck,
"It won't be long now before I lose my neck."
"Be quiet," hushed the cat, "I'm having a nap,
The shooter's asleep, and I'm on his lap."

Well, the shooter awoke, and all was in order.
The cow being milked by the maid in the parlour,
The pig was wallowing in a pool of cool mud,
The dog was chewing on a bone he dug up,
The hens were clucking, and the cat gave a purr,
The shooter was now softly stroking her fur.
So, all was as it should be on the owner's estate.
Animals don't talk. Maybe the occasional debate.

The Song of Paul's Secret

Paul had kept this secret all his life,
No one would ever know.
But a problem shared is a problem halved,
So, Paul decided that at last,
He'd let his lifetime burden go.

His closest friend he chose to tell,
Asking, "Can you keep a secret?
If I share it with you now,
Then you must surely vow
Never, ever to repeat it."

"Of course, of course," was the reply,
"My lips are sealed together,
Unload your woe,
And I will show,
That I'm your friend forever."

So, Paul spoke out his story,
His pain was plain to see.
"We've been good friends all our days,
And this can show in many ways,
Your secret is safe with me."

But the burden became too much to bear,
As years went by with nothing said.
Then he made the fateful choice,
In a desolate spot with a quiet voice,
Spoke the secret to which he was wed.

The secret travelled on the breeze,
And listening were the forest trees,
Who passed it to each other.
From one onto another,
With the rustling of the leaves.

Now common knowledge in woods throughout,
A secret it was no more,
And when all the trees,
Had told all the leaves,
They floated to the floor.

Lying there all winter long,
Quite still upon the grass,
But the secret spread like a weed,
Through flower and seed,
Then the animals began to ask.

"Tell us this secret that can't be kept,"
And soon they knew it all.
Passed it on to humankind,
And inevitably we find,
The news got back to Paul.

I can keep a secret,
It's those I tell who just cannot,
So, I won't take the blame,
That Paul right up until this day,
With broken heart had gone away,
And was never seen again.

Pirates

It was early one morning,
And the ship was just mooring
Looking battered, beaten and old.
It had sailed far and wide,
Some crew members had died
To bring back what was deep in the hold.

The year 1700,
Ships were being plundered
By pirates and countries at war.
So a dangerous quest
That bought some success,
Left the crew just wanting some more.

So, after a time
Of women and wine,
The ship was re-fitted and ready.
The sails did unfold,
and the crew young and old
Shouted, "Steady boys, steady boys, steady!"

The wind filled the sail,
Feeling they cannot fail
Sea shanties were sung by the crew.
Optimism was high,
No clouds in the sky,
What the future held
Nobody knew.

The wind became strong
It wasn't that long
More than a month,
But not more than two.
They were in warmer seas,
Scrubbing decks on their knees.
The sky still a bright shade of blue.

Now the peace didn't last
'Cos high in the mast,
In the crow's nest,
Stood Dead Eyed Big Jim.
Left eye with a patch, but ready to catch
A share of the bounty for him.

Jim was now certain,
That on the horizon
He'd spotted a merchant ship's sail.
"Ship ahoy!', was his call
Heard by them all,
And soon they were close on its tail.

"Ahoy there, me beauties,
Let's get to our duties,"
Said the captain with a voice just like thunder.
"That ship is too slow, and we'll deliver a blow,
It's loaded with riches to plunder.

Now keep her steady,
With ropes at the ready."
All quiet, they had nothing to say.
They came alongside
Thinking just of the prize
Surely theirs, by the end of the day.

So this was the morn
With cutlasses drawn,
Every man had always prepared for.

And with blood in their eyes,
Seeing only the prize,
Each man was prepared now to die for.

The battle was short,
The captain was caught,
And the dead were thrown over the side.
The load was transferred,
Then they all said a word,
For the comrades who that day had died.

The pirates were lenient, and thought it convenient
To leave the merchant ship
With what was left of its men.
A skeleton crew should just ought
Sail back to the port,
And start the process all over again.

So with a gutful of rum,
And a beat of the drum,
The pirates sailed off in full voice.
A life spent at sea,
They were happy to be,
This life was a pirate's first choice.

But this life could not last,
As one day by the mast,
Their last time together they'd spend.
They all would be hung,
All together they swung,
Into history they sailed in the end.

Down the Lane

To pull a crowd he started to shout
This would-be, amiable, street-vending tout.
"What costs you pounds, won't cost you shillings,
What costs you shillings, won't cost you pence.
'Cos here today, I have a bargain.
How can I do it? Well, it just don't make sense.

Your appetite I've whet, starting with this giftset,
Four bath-cubes and some toilet water.
Now the price, you'll think I'm bluffing,
It's a gift from to you from me.
Hard to believe it'll cost you nothing."

With small talk, he carried on
Gathered a throng,
Then offered a scent called 'Torment'.
"This smells of roses and lingers,
I tell you when men take a sniff,
You'll wrap them around your little fingers.

It's another gift for you from me.
Cost you nothing, once again it's all free.
This must be your lucky day.
None of this can be reserved,
It's first come and first served.
You'll regret it, if you walk away.

So here is the last Fabrique D'Or.
A perfume, you'll know it for sure.
Count up what you've got,
All three take away,
Nothing else for me to say,
'Cept, it's a fiver for the whole jolly lot!"

Voices in the crowd were then raised,
Watching it you'd be amazed.
It was selling hand over fist.
But these people were all taken in.
They'd take it home, try it out
Then throw it straight into the bin.

The labels were false,
It was useless of course,
Nothing in this world is ever for free.
As the man in the van,
Who was selling this scam
Was nobody other than me!

THOUGHTS AND RAMBLINGS

These poems are quite personal and not everybody will agree with them. It's just my state of mind when I write them. Sometimes my wife tells me I'm getting too philosophical, but hey, that's just me!

If and Ands

If ifs and ands were pots and pans
There'd be no need of tinkers.
If life was simple and you had it planned,
There'd be no need of thinkers.
I think, therefore they say I am
But I think and I'm confused. Life is sometimes just a scam.
I smile and I'm amused.

So I take each day as it comes.
Win some, lose some, that just it
Don't sit and try to do the sums,
You'll make no sense of it.

Just enjoy each day, and always try
To do the best you can.
Sometimes laugh, and sometimes cry.
Be happy with the race you ran.

The Mayfly

It was the dawn of a new day,
And a mayfly fluttered past.
It turned, I thought I heard it say,
"Live each one, like it's your last."

I turned, replied, "That's quite profound."
The mayfly shook his head.
"Born this morning, I have found
That tonight I will be dead."

So, as the mayfly flew away,
I sat to contemplate,
How to make the most of the day,
Before it was too late.

Of what he said, I was aware,
I knew that much, I oughta.
And then I spied him floating there,
Dead upon the water.

I am my car

Cars are for transport, or to export
You to a place, put a smile on your face.
Touch and you admire, drive and you aspire
To being king of your small court.

An exaggeration, but not a lot
There's elements of truth - as in your youth
Your car is a symbol, what you try to kindle,
You're on the road, heading to the top.

Then it becomes just a tool.
A job to do, just like you.
Sits outside, now gone the pride.
It's for work, family, dog and all.

Before you know it, middle years go by.
Midlife-crisis, is that arthritis?!
Reminiscing, time's now missing,
Open top sport, you think you'll buy.

Stay in that place, or wanting more?
Financially sound, so know no bounds.
Show some clout, that's what it's about,
With that gleaming four by four.

All those cars since you bought your first,
Now the last, which won't go fast.
Off for a rest, dressed in your best,
A passenger in a shiny hearse.

The Demon Drink

The demon drink can make you think
Your words are deep and wise.
But as you seek for those words to speak,
It's telling you some lies.

Thoughts just flow, and on you go.
Ramblings that you decant.
You start transmitting but not receiving.
You sit there and just rant.

Next you see your stability
Desert you when you stand.
You still think, as into a stupor you sink
That you have the upper hand.

Not walking straight, but it's too late
The drink has got its hold.
You laugh, you smile, sit for a while
Then have one for the road.

You've had too much, and now you clutch
To what senses you have left.
Stumbling onto your bed, euphoria gone, now instead
All rational thoughts bereft.

As you awake, again that mistake,
Head pounds, you try to think.
That friend, now the enemy, and the only remedy
Is unfriend that demon drink.

Time passes, you recover and feel you'd like another.
You'll just have one or two.
But soon you slip into its grip,
It has a hold on you.

You can be strong, you know it's wrong,
Slip into another low.
More discipline, then you can win.
Try it! Have a go!

Sometimes I Like to Sit

Sometimes I like to sit and think
But most times I just like to sit.
'Cos when I think, I get confused.
And can make no sense of it.

Round and round in circles,
Trying to work it out.
Come to a conclusion one day,
And the next day start to doubt.

Philosophers through the ages,
Have tried to understand.
What makes us what we are,
This complicated man.

So, my theory is, keep it simple.
Don't try to work it out.
Enjoy each day God gives you.
That's what life is all about.

Life's Goal

Whatever else you think or do
Make happiness your daily task.
Abandon yourself to the joy of laughter
And in its pleasure, wallow and bask.

Condemn the evil of the world.
Remember not all is that way.
Women still find joy in their men,
And somewhere children are at play.

Man's many paths will find refuge
While treading with restless feet.
Passing through the storms of this life.
And in the cheerful house of love will meet.

Self-Image

I look in the mirror and what do I see?
An image of someone who looks just like me.
A man in his prime, not troubled by time.
I hold in my stomach and push out my chest.
I'm in a slim-fit shirt, and still looking my best.
But is this reflection a welcome deception?
I look once again and the image that's there
Is someone who stoops, is losing their hair.
Don't want to see it, don't want to believe it.
Wrinkles and creases and sagging of skin,
Ravages of time, I know I can't win.

So what can I do, when I know it is true?
I've got my health, I'm still on my feet.
I feel and my heart does not miss a beat.
Don't need to impress when I take off my vest.
My character, that's something that needs to be worked on,
So loved ones will remember one day when I'm gone.
Not by my fitness, not by my size
But by the thoughtfulness and love in my eyes.

So time is short, and there's hard work ahead,
To change what's important inside of my head.
Beauty is only as deep as your skin,
Time to bring to the surface what's deeper within.
Time to focus my gaze, it all becomes clear,
To make a difference in the time that I'm here.
Not with my body that's falling apart,
But with the feelings I have in my heart.
I look in the mirror and what do I see?
A man who is smiling looking straight back at me.

My Safe Harbour

In the evening of my day
As the sun sinks in my sky
Sweet memories I can relay
As time has passed me by.

Pleasures that can now be found
Not in frantic, hot pursuit.
Feet planted safely on the ground
I contemplate a tranquil route.

A smile, there's joy upon my face
I watch the world fly past.
I've finished it, I've run my race
I nailed my colours to the mast.

Colours with a softer hue
A time of peaceful reflection.
No longer worry what I say or do
Bask in sweet delectation.

Not striving for 'forever young'
This is my pot of gold.
The stress of life, and work now gone
Enjoying now before I'm really old.

Mortality we all must face
Fruit will rot and fall from the tree.
A marathon or a short-run race
Ripe old age? What will be will be.

I conclude I'm at my best.
Three score and ten, I'm in my prime.
To live and laugh 'til I take my rest.
And my sun sets and it is my time.

A Little Love Poem

They say it's in the eyes of the beholder,
The first time I met you, I knew.
Just standing there,
With your long auburn hair,
Nothing else mattered, all I wanted was you.

Two together are stronger than one it's been said,
And we make the perfect pair.
And as man, I've done all I can,
To make a good life we can share.

Life with you has been something quite special,
And I just wanted to say,
That even with creases my love never ceases,
It'll get stronger and stronger each day.

Now years have passed since I met you,
They've gone in the wink of an eye.
But beauty to me, is something I see,
Not something that you can just buy.

I never want any other,
My past is forgotten right now.
You and I are together,
It will be our forever,
Ad every day I'll remember our vow.

So, thank you for being my special love,
When I went down on one knee.
Taking life's ride with you by my side,
A luckier man there can't be.

Remembering Not to Forget

Do you choose to forget,
Or just not to remember?
I sit and ponder these two words,
My thoughts I shall now tender.

I try to keep things in my head,
Not remembering is not my choice.
So, logically it's involuntary,
And this I clearly voice.

But I forget things all the time,
And that I also do not choose.
So, forget and not remember are the same,
On this point I now sit and muse.

To remember takes an effort,
An interest in what's been said.
To forget is an affliction,
Because it's somewhere in my head.

So, when I forget to remember,
(And I do it quite a lot),
It's not that I'm not interested,
It's because... Oh dear! I just forgot!

Season's Greetings

I hope you're sitting comfortably,
Resting in your favourite chair,
These are thoughts of Christmas,
Which I'd really like to share.

The advent calendar full of chocolate,
The Christmas season just begun,
But by the middle of December,
You've eaten every one!

It's the thought, we're told, that counts,
All wrapped up in a fancy box,
I open mine on Christmas Day,
It's pants, and socks with spots.

Postage stamps cost far too much,
So cards you do not send.
Set aside a few just in case,
You get one from a friend.

Whose turn is it to host this year?
Your house? Or is it theirs?
Will the table be big enough?
Do you have that many chairs?

Decorations from the loft,
What box are they all in?
Spend the day untangling them,
And throw half in the bin.

A real tree, now, that makes a change.
Got a bargain down the market,
But by the time the day arrives,
Half of it's on the carpet.

Last minute shopping, what have you forgot?
What else have you to do?
You head off to the supermarket,
Most of town is in the queue.

The day arrives, the table's set,
You've remembered everything.
Gaze upon the festive spread,
A feast fit for a king.

Talking of which, it's 3pm,
Let's listen to the royal word,
No longer a message from Elizabeth 2,
But Charles, and he's the third.

You sit and watch the same repeats,
Paper hat still on your head,
Altogether it's been good fun,
And now it's time for bed.

What if....?

'What if' is just wishful thinking,
'What if' is just a pointless dream,
'What if' the grass over that fence,
Was really a brighter green?

'What if' there is no pot of gold,
Where the rainbow meets the ground?
'What if' there was no Santa Claus,
Doing his annual round?

But 'what if' can give you hope,
A chance of something new.
'What if' offers imagination,
'What if' to see you through.

There are always two sides to a coin,
Wise words already spoken,
Let's leave it all alone,
Don't fix what isn't broken.

Hindsight

Different paths in life we take,
Each hoping that it will make
A life we'll find fulfilling.

But what we know when our light goes out,
Would be a help, there is no doubt,
If we knew that at the beginning.

Sonnet 1

My mind wanders back to when we were both young
When we were carefree and life just begun.
Enjoying each other, hearts racing, such fun
Together forever, in the warm summer sun
Entwined in embrace, not two, but just one.
A prize to each other, we knew we'd both won.
Now that time has passed and years have gone by,
I gaze at you through a lens in my eye
As together in that same sun we lie.
Joyous contentment, satisfied and I sigh
Don't want it to end, a tear falls, I cry.
Time will pass, surely, one day I will die.
When that day comes and we're no longer together
Wherever I've gone, I'll love you forever.

All Things Considered

All things considered, life is okay.
Some pros and some cons, I'd like to relay.
The smell of grass that's just had a cut,
Rushing to the Post Office and finding it shut.
A new love you meet and your very first kiss.
The 47 bus that you run for and miss.
Welcomed home by your dog's wagging tail.
Monday morning post, full of junk mail.
Cobwebs with pearly droplets of dew.
Stand at the supermarket in the wrong queue.
Family and friends around the table together,
Wishing for sun but getting bad weather.
A flickering flame on a cold winter's night.
Your favourite outfit, now a little too tight.
So, all things considered life is not bad.
Think of the good things in the day you've just had.

A Memory Aide

You forgot such a lot and was told you would not
If you could obtain a brain you could train.
Transplant to enhance, what is the chance?
An idea that sounds queer I think I can hear.
Begin with discipline and you can then win
All that I ask is just bask in the task.
Settle down, don't frown and you'll wear the crown.
You were crazy and lazy, away with the fairies.
But I say, don't dismay, there is another way.
Oh, I have your attention, so an invention I'll mention,
No need to hurry, or study, this is your buddy.
It's easy, believe me, just ask it, it's Siri.

Life Itself

Life itself is a finite thing.
A beginning, a middle and then comes the end.
On that path, where do you sit?
And what do you think and make of it?

Your opinion will change as you move along,
Through quarries of toil and meadows of song.
Seas that are rough and flights that are smooth,
Lost in a forest, or up high with a view.

All things change, nothing stays the same.
Sometimes you lose, sometimes you gain.
You walk on this path, starts when you're born.
From babe-in-arms, to bent over and worn.

Life's journey we're on is not a straight road.
We all carry baggage whatever the load.
So live and let live; each to their own.
We each bear the fruit of the seed we have sown.

No Sooner Said than Done

A human being, or a human doing?
I am my father's son.
Just give me a task,
And as soon as you ask,
It's no sooner said than done.

Once in my head to my hands it will spread,
Relaxing just not on the agenda.
As I work out the way
To achieve what you say,
I'm a fixer, repairer, a mender.

Jack-of-all-trades, master of none,
But I'll give it a go anyway.
Sometimes it works,
Sometimes it hurts,
Will there be more minor injuries today?

I give it my best, I cannot rest,
'Til this job at hand is complete.
Then I look for another,
No time to recover,
Even feeling quite dead on my feet.

Slow down, take your time, I hear in my mind,
Walk, there's no need to run.
Teach an old dog new tricks.
No time, off to Wicks!
And it's no sooner said, than done.

A. I.

Can A.I. write a poem?
Can A.I. write a song?
I'm told that it can do it all,
But it somehow just sounds wrong.

It doesn't have a soul,
It doesn't have a heart.
There's something else that's missing,
I can tell it from the start.

Machines can do a lot of things,
Of that I must agree.
But emotion? Just forget it.
A. I. cannot copy me.

Life needs to be lived,
With all its ups and downs.
Not made up of algorithms
Meaningless verbs and pointless nouns.

A.I. is really no competition,
So, I shall now relax.
You lack a spirit, my sad machine.
You really are no match.

With my fingers on the keyboard,
Uninstall, and you're defeated.
Don't need your cold and heartless words.
Not wanted, you're deleted.

Inspired by hearing in February 2022, that ChatGPT could write an
essay or – worse still – a poem.

Secrets

Can you keep a secret?
Can you always lock it
Somewhere safe and secure,
And not just in your pocket?

I can keep a secret.
It's the people I tell that just cannot.
They don't have any willpower,
But then, I don't have a lot.

So, take this one to the grave,
No matter what's been said.
As two can keep a secret,
If one of them is dead!

The Garden

The garden is not a place just for you
To sit, relax and enjoy the view.
But a home to a variety of life.
So, where it's overgrown, don't have a moan
Smile, don't sit with a frown,
As somewhere out there – be happy to share,
It's a beasties' two up and two down.

it's certainly not a waste,
To give nature some space.
Somewhere it can do its own thing.
As a manicured garden, well, I do beg your pardon,
What's wrong with a few natural weeds?
Add tarmac and concrete, it might look quite neat,
But not for the birds and the bees.

So don't concrete it over,
Leave the grass with some clover.
Some wildflowers - a bonus for all.
Some old, rotting wood, well, it really just could
Be an animals' neat pied-a-terre.
And birds will sing as they fly on the wing.
Your garden is somewhere to share.

Eye Contact

Don't stare! I was always taught
It's a bad habit that you ought
Not to let become the norm.
An anti-social thing to do,
As it could become the cue
To stir up and unwanted storm.

Who you looking at?!
Feel the start of an attack,
Back-off or stand your ground?
You think twice,
An altercation won't be nice,
Probably best to turn around.

Be silent and don't say a word,
The situation's getting absurd.
You just craved a stranger's smile.
But people look the other way,
Don't need this to start their day,
Could all just get hostile.

You ponder this and wonder why,
You look around and catch another eye.
Receive a smile and not a frown.
Being still as your eyes meet,
You stand and offer them your seat.
Alight next stop, it's Camden Town.

Proverbs

You can lead a horse to water,
But you cannot make him drink.
You can tell a man what to do,
But you cannot make him think.
What goes up, must come down,
One in the hand is worth two in the bush.
If you want to open a door,
Sometimes you must give it a push.
He who hesitates will be lost,
But look before you leap.
Actions speak much louder than words,
What you sew, so shall you reap.
Faint heart never won fair maiden,
So, keep your eye on the ball.
Better to have loved and lost,
Than never to have loved at all.
A change, so we've been told,
Is just as good as a rest.
And a dead bird, so we all know,
Will never leave its nest.
Act in haste and you'll repent in leisure,
I'm confused at which way to go.
Welcome to my world,
And tell me if you know.

A Life in Numbers

Remember at 10 a time without thought,
And life was all about play?

Remember at 20 you felt so free,
And the night melted into the day?

Remember at 30 it seemed so old,
You thought that you knew it all?

Remember at 40 when life should begin,
You're trying to stay on the ball?

Remember at 50 some wrinkles? Going grey?
Have the best years already passed?

Remember at 60 disbelieving the number,
And feeling it's all gone too fast?

Remember at 70 starting to feel old,
Aches and pains just don't go away?

Remember at 80 you've started to bend,
And slower at starting your day?

Remember at 90 and you are worn out,
Life really isn't much fun?

Forget at 100 it's all been and gone,
Lights out and your time is done.

Not my World

I'm old fashioned for sure,
You might call me a bore,
Or nostalgic, if you so wish.
But it's all gone wrong,
This path that we're one,
On the menu, there's no other dish.

The weather's all wrong,
The seasons have gone,
A tsunami, a quake or a drought.
We contaminate the air,
And don't seem to care,
The planet is looking worn out.

Now you have found,
There's no jobs to go around.
Bills getting harder to pay.
Land is all built on,
No grass just to sit on,
The high street in a state of decay.

Now just take a look,
There won't be a book.
You spend all your day online.
Is everyone having fun,
While you're having none?
No, we're all just wasting our time.

On social media there's pressure,
As you sit there at leisure.
Maybe a facelift, or even a tuck.
Try to all look the same,
That's the name of the game.
If you can't, well, that's just hard luck.

We'll be putting our gender
Straight through a blender.
A man, a woman, a them or a they.
One day a shirt, the next day a skirt.
Don't want to upset, don't know what to say.

Leave your keys on the shelf,
You won't drive yourself,
The car will just take you there.
Your own sterile bubble,
Can't cause any trouble,
Do as you're told, rebel if you dare.

Stock market will crash,
There'll be no more cash.
Just a card, so they know what you buy.
It's yours, you can have it,
And all that is in it.
I hand it over, I'm sorry, Goodbye.

Opposites Attract

You do it this way, I do it that.
You wear a scarf; I wear a hat.
You wear walking shoes; I wear a welly.
I'll play some music; you'll watch the telly.
You on your own, no company's just fine.
I like more company; I don't like mine.
I like the heat; you like the cold.
You're feeling young; I'm feeling old.
When I say yes, you'll say no.
When I want to stop, you'll have a go.
When I say it's red, you'll say it's blue.
Why on earth am I staying with you?!
Because I love you, that's why
Please agree or at least try.

I hasten to add this is not about me and my nearest and dearest!

The following is another poem inspired by the Poets with Parkinson's group. One of the monthly challenges was to write a poem about a pre-decimal penny coin, 1D for those who can remember that far back.

The Old Penny

"What were you worth back in the day?"
I asked the old penny that was there on display.
And offered her one for whatever she thought.
Britannia was there just on one side,
Looked at me sadly, and then she replied,
"Here's just a few of the things that I bought.

A book of matches, a bargain to buy.
In November, one was enough for the guy.
In amusement arcades I could always be found,
If you gamble with me in a bandit's slot,
A pile came out when you won the jackpot.
There were 240 to make up a pound.

You could buy four blackjacks for only a penny,
And if, by chance, you didn't have any,
For a farthing you could buy just the one.
The blackjack eventually changed its name,
As nothing ever stays the same,
Decimalisation arrived, and we were undone."

You looked after your pennies and the pound was OK,
And under their breath your neighbour would say,
"A pretty penny – well that wasn't cheap."
'I need to spend a penny', and everyone knew,
Nature was calling and you needed the loo.
Much more polite than saying "I need a leak."

So, finally the penny was abandoned and died,
When on the scene the new pence arrived.
No longer a coin that you could invest,
With a ten bob note and threepenny bit.
Half-crown and shilling, that was it.
Your destiny a display case, laid to rest.

Ebbs and Flows

All life's non-volitional motion,
Are characterized by rhythm, so here is my notion.
Why do we thrive on a daily routine?
Cos we know where we're going and we knew where we've been,
Watching the tide as it ebbs and flows.
First coming in and then out it goes.
The sun comes up and the sun goes down,
Every day is the same, going round and around.
It's happening everywhere, just take a look,
So, let's take a leaf from the earth's clever book.
When things are going wrong and nothing seems right,
Apply the same principle and I think that it might,
Show you the path to enjoying each day.
The earth in its wisdom can show you the way.
So, with that thought kept in your head,
On bad days don't fight it, just think that instead,
What goes up will eventually come down,
And what's gone around will again come round.
Life is just circles, nothing new under the sun.
Whatever you do has already been done.
Worry will just take you nearer the grave.
So, when by the sea and watching the waves,
Meditate on how it ebbs, and it flows,
Always coming in, and then out it goes,
If today's going wrong, don't condemn in a hurry,
Today is the tomorrow that was yesterday's worry.

Up and Down

It's not how you fall, it's how you rise.
That's the truth, don't listen to lies.
When the sun's not rising, and all is just rain
When the wall is too high, and you just want to cry
Pick yourself up and start over again.

Times can be good, times can be bad,
Sometimes you're happy and sometimes you're sad.
And sometimes you just need a lift.
But this life that is yours, whether it's quiet, or roars
Is a God-given, wonderful gift.

Queen Elizabeth II died on 8th September 2022. It was a monumental event in not only my life, but that of the country. I had lived almost exactly all my life with her as my monarch having been born just a year prior to her accension to the throne. These poems are my humble tribute.

The Queen is Dead

The Queen has gone, we sing a song
Of sadness and farewells
Along with the shock, we sit, take stock
As toll the countries bells.

Such long stability, we know we shall see
On another hand the royal ring
The Queen is dead, and it must be said
Together, long live the King.

E motionally we say goodbye,
L ife ends and at peace you lie,
I n royal state to rest at last,
Z enith reached and sadly passed,
A duty complete and now it's finished,
B lazing light has now diminished,
E lizabeth the second, our lifelong queen,
T he journey over, this was your fate,
H istory will surely call you great.

Notes on Parkinson's

Parkinson's is a progressive neurological condition for which there is currently no cure. The condition develops when nerve cells that are responsible for producing a chemical known as dopamine die. Dopamine allows messages to be sent to the parts of the brain that coordinate movement. With the loss of dopamine-producing nerve cells, these parts of the brain are unable to work normally, causing symptoms of Parkinson's to appear.

In the UK, more than 153,000 people are currently living with Parkinson's. With population growth and ageing, it is estimated that this will increase to around 172,000 people in the UK by 2030. There is currently no cure for Parkinson's but there are lots of different treatments, therapies and support available to help manage the condition.

Parkinson's doesn't directly cause people to die, but symptoms do get worse over time and life expectancy is shortened. There are more than 40 symptoms of the condition, but Parkinson's affects everyone differently.

I've incorporated some of my own symptoms in the following poems:

Last Night I had a Dream
REM Sleep Behaviour Disorder is a condition during which the patient experiences vivid, often violent dreams which they can act out sometimes harming themselves or their sleeping partner. Sleep Behaviour Disorder often precedes Parkinson's by some years and is seen as an early indicator.

Insomnia
People with Parkinson's can be more prone to insomnia because of Parkinson's symptoms, such as tremor, stiffness, pain and restless leg syndrome that can all disturb sleep. Also, some medications can act as stimulants and keep the sufferer awake.

Horns of Uncertainty
Anxiety is a feeling of unease, such as worry or fear, which some people with Parkinson's experience. Constant worry, difficulty concentrating, and

indecision are all features of anxiety that are hard to cope with on a daily basis.

No Choice
With Parkinson's the lack of Dopamine can be a trigger for depression. Combined with apathy, fatigue and anxiety living with an incurable brain condition can have a serious impact on your mental health.

Living the Dream
Half of people with Parkinson's experience extreme fatigue which affects both physical and mental function. Learning to pace activities, avoiding stress and building in recovery time can all help.

Relatively Speaking
Parkinson's can affect the muscles of the throat, which can make swallowing difficult. Parkinson's is a disease which effects the autonomic system (the things we do without thinking: blinking, swallowing, breathing), so Parkinson's sufferers often dribble – producing the same amount of saliva, but not swallowing. Chewing gum can help.

Parkinson's sufferers also loose facial expression and must be reminded to smile. One of my early symptoms was when my wife noticed I had stopped smiling in photographs. This is called flat face, or masking.

ACKNOWLEDGEMENTS

Thank you to my children, Leon, Lisa and Carla. It has been the pleasure of my life to see you grow into the wonderful people you have become. And also, to my grandchildren, Alex, Anna, Raiffe and Connie. I can't wait to see what happens in your lives.

I would like to thank my good friend and fellow poet Peter Norman for his input and his encouragement on my poetic journey.

Also, my thanks to the Poets with Parkinson's family for their friendship and camaraderie in our battle against this insidious disease. With them I feel less alone.

Special thanks to Martin Pickard, from whom I 'borrowed' the Notes on Parkinson's section. Reading his book of poetry *The Shaken Word* has encouraged me to publish my own collection.

My love and thanks to Arthur, our Schnoodle, for just being you. Everyone thinks their dog is the best, and everyone's right.

And finally, the one person I can't do without, my wife Bridget, who not only typed all this up, but also listens to my constant ramblings of half-finished and half thought-out poems!

Thank you to you for buying this book. We are donating the profits to Parkinson's UK. Thank you for your contribution. You've made a difference.

Printed in Great Britain
by Amazon

53664942R10050